Michel Roux

DESSERTS

TEN RECIPES

Michel Roux

DESSERTS

TEN RECIPES

WEIDENFELD & NICOLSON

MICHEL ROUX's delicious desserts have made him famous throughout the world. He began his career as a pastry chef apprentice at the Pâtisserie Loyal in Paris, and then worked for the British Embassy in Paris and for Mlle Cecile de Rothschild.

With his brother, Albert, he opened Le Gavroche in London in 1967. The Waterside Inn at Bray in Berkshire opened in 1972 and since then has consistently won many major international gastronomy awards. It is one of only two restaurants in the country to hold Michelin's top accolade of three stars. Michel Roux was awarded Meilleur Ouvrier de France en Pâtisserie in 1976 and received the Chevalier de l'Ordre National du Mérite in 1986 and the Chevalier de l'Ordre des Arts et des Lettres in 1990.

With Albert, he has written several books, including *New Classic Cuisine* (1983), *Roux Brothers on Pâtisserie* (1986), *At Home with the Roux Brothers* (1988), which accompanied a BBC television series, *French Country Cooking* (1989), *Cooking for Two* (1991). He has also published *Desserts – A Lifelong Passion* (1994) and *Only the Best* (2002).

CONTENTS

Maybe I am biased, because I began my career as a pastry chef, but I consider dessert to be one of the most important parts of a meal, like the final act of a play. It need not be a complicated assembly of different elements: a refined dessert may be simple and elegant, and a well-made old favourite will always be welcome.

I have chosen these ten desserts to be both varied and visually appealing: Pear and Ginger Sabayon a mountain of pale foam; Chocolate Crème Brûlée with a deep golden surface, hard and shiny as a mirror; Creamy Apple Mousse spiked with apple crisps to resemble a hedgehog. A soufflé is an exciting way to end a meal, and really not difficult – try it once or twice and you will soon gain confidence. Of course, a soufflé must be cooked just before serving, but there are plenty of ideas for desserts that can be made in advance: pure-tasting Raspberry Ice Cream; Blackberry Clafoutis, a variation on a French country classic; and Choux Puffs, light as a cloud and filled with fresh summer berries.

'I consider dessert to be one of the most important parts of a meal, like the final act of a play.'

'The dessert, being the last course of the meal, must always be the most exciting part, and therefore needs to be light and delicate to encourage the palate to be tempted further.'

RECIPES

serves 8
250 g/9 oz quick puff pastry (page 35)
4 eggs
200 g/7 oz caster sugar
25 g/1 oz flour

125 ml/4 fl oz milk
125 ml/4 fl oz double cream
2 tablespoons kirsch (optional)
250 g/9 oz blackberries
2 tablespoons granulated sugar

BLACKBERRY CLAFOUTIS

On a lightly floured work surface, roll out the pastry to form a circle, 2 mm/$\frac{1}{16}$ inch thick. Use to line a greased, loose-bottomed 24 cm/ 9½ inch diameter tart tin and cut off any excess pastry around the rim. Chill for 20 minutes.

Preheat the oven to 220°C/425°F/Gas Mark 7. Prick the pastry with a fork, line it with greaseproof paper and fill with baking beans. Bake blind for 20 minutes, then remove from the oven; remove the beans and paper. Reduce the oven temperature to 200°C/400°F/Gas Mark 6.

Put the eggs and caster sugar in a bowl, whisk together for 2 minutes, then add the flour and whisk for a further 2 minutes. Still whisking, add the milk, cream and kirsch, if using. Spread the blackberries over the pastry, pour in the cream mixture and bake for 30 minutes or until just set. As soon as the clafoutis is cooked, remove the outside of the tart tin, leaving the clafoutis on the base.

Just before serving, sprinkle the granulated sugar over the barely warm clafoutis.

serves 6
4 egg yolks
50 g/2 oz caster sugar
3 tablespoons cold water

100 ml/3½ fl oz pear eau-de-vie
50 g/2 oz preserved ginger in syrup,
 drained and finely chopped

PEAR AND GINGER SABAYON

First prepare a bain-marie: half-fill with cold water a saucepan large enough to hold the base of a mixing bowl.

Place all the ingredients in the mixing bowl and start whisking with a balloon whisk. Set the base of the bowl in the bain-marie and place over medium heat. Whisk continuously for 10–12 minutes; the temperature of the water in the bain-marie should not exceed 90°C/195°F or the sabayon will start to coagulate. If necessary, turn off or reduce the heat under the pan. Keep whisking until the sabayon becomes glossy and has the consistency of half-risen egg whites. The texture should be unctuous, frothy and light (the temperature should not exceed 55°C/130°F). As soon as the sabayon is ready, stop whisking, spoon it into bowls or large glasses and serve immediately.

serves 4–8 (1 or 2 ramekins each)
5–6 bananas, not too ripe
juice of 2 lemons
150 g/5 oz butter

150 g/5 oz caster sugar
600 g/1¼ lb pastry cream (page 36)
150 ml/¼ pint double cream
6 tablespoons dark rum

BANANA RAMEKINS
WITH CARAMEL TOPPING

Peel the bananas, cut them into 1 cm/½ inch rounds and mix them with
the lemon juice in a bowl.

Heat the butter in a frying pan, sprinkle on 85 g/3 oz of the caster
sugar, add the banana rounds and lightly brown them over high heat for
2 minutes. Transfer to a plate and set aside.

In a bowl, whisk together the pastry cream, double cream and rum.
Place a spoonful of this cream into each of eight small ramekins, about
9 cm/3½ inches in diameter.

Reserve the eight best banana rounds for decoration, then divide the
rest between the ramekins. Fill up the ramekins with the cream, smooth
the surface with a palette knife and sprinkle the tops with the remaining
caster sugar. Caramelize the sugar with a blowtorch or under a very hot
salamander or grill. Place two ramekins on each plate and garnish each
ramekin with a reserved banana round. Serve at once.

serves 6
400 g/14 oz fresh or frozen raspberries
100 ml/3½ fl oz cold water
200 g/7 oz caster sugar
juice of 2 lemons

3 tablespoons raspberry eau-de-vie or
    kirsch (optional)
300 ml/½ pint double cream, whipped
    to a ribbon consistency

RASPBERRY ICE CREAM

Purée the raspberries with the water in a liquidizer for 2 minutes. Pass the purée through a wire-mesh conical sieve into a large bowl, rubbing and pushing it through with the back of a ladle.

Add the sugar to the resulting raspberry juice, then add the lemon juice and eau-de-vie or kirsch, if using, and whisk together. Fold in the cream, transfer the mixture to an ice-cream maker and churn for about 15 minutes or until the ice cream is velvety and half-frozen. Transfer to a bowl and freeze, or serve immediately.

Blackberries can be substituted for the raspberries.

serves **4**

350 g/13 oz quick puff pastry (page 35)
150 g/5 oz granulated sugar
500 ml/16 fl oz water
4 very ripe peaches, skinned

eggwash (1 egg white mixed with
  1 tablespoon milk)
40 g/1½ oz icing sugar
1 tablespoon grenadine syrup

WARM PEACH FEUILLETÉS

On a lightly floured work surface, roll out the pastry to about 5 mm/ ¼ inch thick. Using a 9 cm/3½ inch pastry cutter, cut out four circles and place them on a baking sheet lightly moistened with cold water. Chill for 20 minutes.

Place the granulated sugar and the water in a saucepan and bring to the boil over low heat, stirring occasionally until the sugar has dissolved. Add the peaches and poach until just tender. Using a slotted spoon, lift the peaches out of the syrup; reserve the syrup.

Preheat the oven to 220°C/425°F/Gas Mark 7. Brush the tops of the pastry circles with eggwash. Lightly press a 7 cm/2¾ inch pastry cutter on to the circles to mark out the lids. With the tip of a knife, score criss-crosses on the lids.

Bake the pastry circles in the oven for 10 minutes, then sprinkle them with the icing sugar and bake for another 2–3 minutes, until the sugar forms an attractive glaze.

Slide the pastry circles on to a wire rack. Run the tip of a knife around the marked lids and detach them carefully, lifting them off with the knife.

Put 85 ml/3 fl oz of the poaching syrup and the grenadine in a small saucepan and simmer over low heat until reduced by half.

Place a peach in each pastry case and put them on individual plates. Lightly coat the peaches with the reduced syrup and arrange the lids aslant at the edge of the pastry cases. Serve at once.

serves 8
300 g/11 oz bitter couverture or
    best-quality plain dark chocolate
    (about 64% cocoa solids)
500 ml/16 fl oz milk

500 ml/16 fl oz double cream
3 tablespoons liquid glucose
8 egg yolks
150 g/5 oz caster sugar

CHOCOLATE
CRÈME BRÛLÉE

Break the chocolate into a large bowl and sit the bowl over a saucepan half-filled with hot water. Leave to melt, stirring occasionally until smooth.

Place the milk, cream and liquid glucose in a saucepan and bring to the boil over low heat, whisking occasionally.

In a bowl, whisk the egg yolks with 50 g/2 oz of the sugar until just pale.

Whisking continuously, pour the boiling milk mixture on to the melted chocolate. When it is thoroughly combined, pour the mixture on to the egg yolk mixture, whisking all the time.

Preheat the oven to 90°C/195°F/Gas Mark ¼. Divide the chocolate cream mixture between eight gratin dishes, about 15 cm/6 inches in diameter, and cook for 40 minutes or until just set.

Slide the dishes on to a wire rack and leave to cool at room temperature. Place in the refrigerator for a very short time.

Just before serving, sprinkle 2 teaspoons caster sugar evenly over each crème brûlée and caramelize with a blowtorch or under a very hot salamander or grill. Place each one on a plate and serve at once.

The contrast between the warm, crunchy topping and the lightly chilled cream is delicious. To reach the cream you will need to tap the top sharply with a spoon to crack it open, as shown in the picture.

serves 6
150 g/5 oz flour
25 g/1 oz caster sugar
pinch of salt
2 eggs
300 ml/½ pint milk

6 tablespoons double cream
clarified butter for cooking the pancakes
400 g/14 oz pastry cream (page 36)
grated zest and juice of 2 oranges, juice
  simmered until reduced by half
40 g/1½ oz icing sugar

SURPRISE ORANGE PANCAKES

Sift the flour into a bowl and mix in the caster sugar and salt. Lightly whisk in the eggs, then the milk, a little at a time. When the mixture is thoroughly combined, stir in the cream, cover with clingfilm and leave the batter to rest for at least 1 hour.

Heat a frying pan, about 30 cm/12 inches in diameter, and brush it with a little clarified butter. Add a ladleful of batter, quickly swirl it around to cover the base of the pan, and cook the pancake for 30 seconds, then turn it over with a palette knife and cook on the other side for 30 seconds. Make more pancakes in this way until all the batter is used; there should be 12 pancakes in all.

Using a whisk, mix the pastry cream with the orange zest and juice. Spread a spoonful of this mixture over each pancake and roll them up. Arrange the filled pancakes on a baking sheet and sprinkle with icing sugar. Glaze them under a very hot salamander or grill, then place two pancakes on each plate, lifting them with a palette knife. Serve at once.

100 g/3½ oz wild or small strawberries
100 g/3½ oz bilberries
100 g/3½ oz redcurrants
250 g/9 oz choux paste (½ quantity, page 37)

250 ml/8 fl oz whipping cream, chilled
40 g/1½ oz icing sugar, plus extra for dusting
1 teaspoon vanilla essence

TUTTI FRUTTI CHOUX PUFFS

Preheat the oven to 220°C/425°F/Gas Mark 7. If necessary, delicately wash and drain the fruit, then hull or top and tail.

Using a piping bag fitted with a plain nozzle, pipe four large choux puffs on to a baking sheet. Dip a fork into cold water and mark the tops lightly with the back of the fork, dipping it into cold water each time. This will help the pastry to develop evenly as it cooks. Bake the puffs for 20 minutes, reducing the oven temperature to 200°C/400°F/Gas Mark 6 after 10 minutes.

When the puffs are cooked, transfer them to a wire rack. Using a serrated knife, cut off a 'hat' four-fifths of the way up each puff.

In a bowl, whip the cream with the icing sugar and vanilla essence until it forms soft peaks. Fill a piping bag fitted with a fluted nozzle with this cream and pipe a small rosette into each puff. Pile a mixture of the fruits into the puffs, then pipe a band of cream around the puffs. Serve at once, or place in the refrigerator for no more than 1 hour before serving, dusted with icing sugar.

serves 4
25 g/1 oz butter, softened
175 g/6 oz caster sugar
3 oranges, peeled and divided into
   segments, all pith and membrane
   removed

300 g/11 oz pastry cream (page 36)
3 tablespoons grand marnier
8 egg whites
4 sprigs of mint
2 tablespoons icing sugar

HOT GRAND MARNIER SOUFFLÉS WITH ORANGE SEGMENTS

Brush the insides of four small soufflé dishes, about 10 cm/4 inches in diameter, with the butter. Tip 25 g/1 oz of the caster sugar into one of the dishes and rotate it so that the interior is well coated. Tip the excess sugar into the next dish and repeat the process with all the dishes.

Preheat the oven to 190°C/375°F/Gas Mark 5 and put in a baking sheet to heat.

Reserve the eight best orange segments for the garnish and cut the remaining segments lengthways into three.

Put the pastry cream into a bowl, stand this in a bain-marie (see page 16) and warm gently. Whisk in the Grand Marnier.

Beat the egg whites with an electric mixer or by hand until half-risen, then add the remaining 150 g/5 oz of caster sugar and beat until the mixture forms soft peaks. Still using the whisk, fold one-third of the egg whites into the pastry cream, then very delicately fold in the rest of the whites, using a spatula.

Half-fill the soufflé dishes with the mixture, divide the cut orange segments between the dishes, then fill them up with soufflé mixture and smooth the surface with a palette knife. Using the tip of a knife, ease the mixture away from the edges of the dishes.

Stand the soufflé dishes on the heated baking sheet and cook in the oven for 7–8 minutes. Arrange two of the reserved orange segments and a mint sprig on each soufflé, dust with icing sugar and serve immediately.

serves 6
600 ml/1 pint apple juice
8 egg yolks
70 g/2½ oz caster sugar
6 gelatine leaves, soaked in cold water,
    then well drained
4 tablespoons calvados
12 tablespoons apple purée

300 ml/½ pint whipping cream
    and 85 g/3 oz icing sugar, whipped
    to soft peaks

apple crisps
4 dessert apples, not too ripe
40 g/1½ oz caster sugar
40 g/1½ oz icing sugar

APPLE HEDGEHOG

Pour the apple juice into a saucepan and simmer to reduce by one-third.

In a bowl, whisk the egg yolks with the caster sugar to a light ribbon consistency. Still whisking, pour the boiling apple juice on to the mixture. Return this to the saucepan and cook over very low heat, without boiling, stirring continuously with a wooden spoon until the custard is thick enough to coat the back of the spoon. Off the heat, stir in the drained gelatine, then pass the custard through a sieve into a bowl. Set aside, stirring from time to time. When almost cold, use a whisk to fold in the Calvados, apple purée and whipped cream. Divide between six moulds, about 10 cm/4 inches in diameter, and place in the freezer for 1 hour, or in the refrigerator for 4 hours, until the mousses are set but not too firm.

Preheat the oven to 180°C/350°F/Gas Mark 4.

For the apple crisps, halve the apples horizontally and use a plain 3 cm/1¼ inch diameter pastry cutter to cut around the core to make cylinders of apple, leaving behind the core and pips. Cut the cylinders into the thinnest possible discs. Spread the discs over a greased baking sheet and sprinkle each with a pinch of caster sugar. Cook for 8 minutes, then turn them over one at a time and cook for a further 4 minutes. Transfer to a wire rack.

Briefly dip the base of each mould into very hot water. With your fingertips, lightly push one side of the mousse and invert the mould on to a serving plate. Poke the apple crisps into the mousses to resemble hedgehog spines and dust with a little icing sugar. Serve at once.

THE BASICS

Makes 1.2 kg/2¾ lb
500 g/1 lb 2 oz flour, plus extra for turning
500 g/1 lb 2 oz firm butter, cut into cubes
  (take out of the refrigerator 1 hour
  before using)

1 teaspoon salt
250 ml/8 fl oz iced water

QUICK PUFF PASTRY

This pastry will rise about 30 per cent less than classic puff pastry, but it is much easier to prepare.

Put the flour on to the work surface or into a bowl, and make a well in the centre. Add the butter and salt to the well. Work the ingredients together using the fingertips of your right hand, gradually drawing in the flour with your left hand.

When the mixture resembles breadcrumbs, pour in the iced water and gradually work it into the pastry, without kneading. When the pastry comes together to form a dough, but still contains small flakes of butter, roll it out on a lightly floured surface, rolling away from you, to form a 40 x 20 cm/16 x 8 inch rectangle.

Fold in the ends, as if folding a letter, to make three equal layers. Turn the pastry through 90 degrees and repeat the rolling process. These are the first two turns. Wrap the pastry in clingfilm and chill in the refrigerator for 30 minutes.

After 30 minutes, take it out of the refrigerator and roll out again, making two more turns. The pastry is now ready. Roll to the required shape, place on a dampened baking sheet and refrigerate for 20 minutes before use.

Alternatively the pastry can be wrapped in clingfilm and stored in the refrigerator.

Makes about 750 g/1 lb 10 oz
6 egg yolks
125 g/4 oz caster sugar
40 g/1½ oz flour
500 ml/16 fl oz milk
1 vanilla pod, split
a little butter or icing sugar

PASTRY CREAM

For coffee or chocolate pastry cream, omit the vanilla pod and use a little instant coffee or cocoa powder, to taste. If using cocoa powder, use a little less flour and a little extra sugar.

In a large bowl, whisk the egg yolks with about one-third of the caster sugar until pale and thick (a light ribbon consistency). Sift the flour over the mixture and mix in thoroughly.

Bring the milk to the boil with the remaining sugar and the vanilla pod. As soon as it begins to bubble, pour one-third into the egg mixture, stirring all the time. Pour back into the saucepan and bring to the boil over a very low heat, stirring all the time. Allow to bubble for 2 minutes, then pour the pastry cream into a bowl. To prevent a skin from forming, dot with a few flakes of butter or dust lightly with icing sugar.

Pastry cream can be stored in the refrigerator for 36 hours.

Makes 22–25 small choux puffs or éclairs
125 ml/4 fl oz water
125 ml/4 fl oz milk
100 g/3½ oz butter, finely diced
½ teaspoon fine salt
¾ teaspoon sugar

150 g/5 oz flour, sifted
4 eggs
eggwash (1 egg yolk mixed with
  2 teaspoons milk and a pinch
  of salt) – optional

CHOUX PASTE

Put the water, milk, butter, salt and sugar into a saucepan and boil over a high heat for 1 minute. Make sure that the mixture is well combined and then remove from the heat. Add the flour at once, stirring with a wooden spoon to make a smooth paste.

Return the pan to the heat and stir for 1 minute. Be careful not to let the paste dry too much or it will crack during cooking. Transfer the paste to a bowl and beat in the eggs one at a time. Beat the paste until very smooth.

If the pastry is not to be used immediately, spread a little eggwash over the surface to prevent a crust from forming.

Choux paste can be stored in an airtight container in the refrigerator for 3 days or in the freezer for up to 1 week.

The Waterside Inn
Ferry Road,
Bray, SL6 2AT
Tel: 01628 620 691
Fax: 01628 784 710

The White Hart Inn
High Street
Nayland
Nr. Colchester
Suffolk
CO6 4JF
Tel: 01206 263 382
Fax: 01206 263 638
E-Mail:
reservations@whitehart-nayland.co.uk

ADDRESSES

This edition first published in 2004 by Weidenfeld & Nicolson
First published in 1996 by Weidenfeld & Nicolson
Text © Michel Roux, 1996, 2004
Food photography © Simon Wheeler, 1996, 2004
Design and layout copyright © Weidenfeld & Nicolson, 2004

Front cover photography by David Jones

A CIP catalogue record for this book is available from the British Library

ISBN 0 297 84366 4

Design director David Rowley
Editorial director Susan Haynes
Project Editor Matt Lowing
Designed by Austin Taylor
Printed and bound in Italy by Printer Trento s.r.l.

Weidenfeld & Nicolson
The Orion Publishing Group
Wellington House
125 Strand
London WC2R 0BB